Clay Tablets In Nietzsche's Cave

Raed Anis Al-Jishi
Preface by
George Elliott Clarke

Cover Image by Naseem Ali Alabduljabar

Edited by Sarah Raine

Published by Sail Publishing L.L.C.

First published in 2021

Copyright © 2021 by Sail Publishing L.L.C.

All rights reserved. This book or any portion thereof may not be reproduced or used in any manner whatsoever without the express written permission of the publisher except for the use of brief quotations in a book review.

The cover was designed by Naseem Ali Alabduljabar

Overall editing done by Sarah Raine

This book uses a font and an alignment purposed to make the reading experience easier for dyslexics, towards an inclusive reading experience.

ISBN: 978-9948-8692-0-7

UAE National Media Council Permit #: MC-02-01-0321184

Age Classification: +16
The age classification for this book's contents is set in accordance with the age classification system issued by the UAE's National Media Council.

Email: info@SailPublishing.com
Facebook: facebook.com/SailPublishing
Instagram: @SailPublishing
Twitter: @SailPublishing

2

Preface:

Clay Tablets in Nietzsche's Cave is a masterful, poetic work--and as momentous for the reception of Arabic poetry in English as was the discovery of the Dead Sea Scrolls for theologians and anthropologists. These "clay tablets"--excavated ostensibly from the cave of the Neanderthal of atheistic philosophy--unfurl a tour-de-force of aphoristic verses insisting on our need to sing, especially in negotiating our existence as animate dust, prostrate before Divinity. Raed Anis Al-Jishi will remind some readers of Rumi. However, his mysticism--if that's what it is-- moves in sympathy with the surrealism of Octavio Paz. The strangeness of his insight always conveys deep feeling: "Your shiver is an outpouring of beauty." In fact, you're "burying yourself with your self." Moreover, "your shadow--as you know-- is your only legacy / to the inheritance of the crucifixion." Al-Jishi's verses--like those of the love-crazed bard, Majnun-- contemplate poetry's eternal defiance of mortality: "drizzle wishes to write your blood's iliad // and feels proud when it reads it / and asks itself: is it really me / who wrote the elegy of bleeding?" In a sense, Al-Jishi tells us, in lines vivid as fire and clear as water, a cave-bound philosopher is always out-thought, out-theologian'd, by the poetry inscribed on the clay--even if broken--tablets flanking the mortal self.

George Elliott Clarke
Parliamentary Poet Laureate of Canada (2016 & 2017)
E.J. Pratt Professor of Canadian LIterature
University of Toronto

Acknowledgements:

To my small family for supporting me all the way, and to Iowa University and all the staff of its International Writing Program for giving me the space, free time, abundant literary resources and positive energy I needed to write this book.

1-Too Young to be Drunk

I draw an "X" on my hand
to say: I will not drink
from the liquor of the dream;
I will not partake in the diversion of drugs ;
I drink no milk with the meat of lust
or sip cold tea with lemon .
As a civilian

I enjoy the music of cawing,
condensed in the click of glass .
I used to call them the wings of the devil.

I don't trust in a trimmed scale ,
constricting like a tomb
hidden by a cinematic crow,
its beak made from glass,
its tongue a cold corpse--
Maybe if I borrow more darkness ;
maybe if I shatter the source of light in the mirrors of Earth ,

maybe if I lash his back with the sun
as hard as a star could practice
its freedom of the press,
I may see him in a face
that won't swindle my thirst .

How many howling dogs should die?
And how many clowns should I heed
when I cross the nonsensical pasture?

Clowns are the wisest and the cruelest.
They laugh at our faces' reflections
and our bashful cries of childish joy.
They tell themselves :
How petty you are!
Petty and tame like circus dogs...
...

2-The Body

With eyes half-closed
and a headache that won't be purged
by aspirin's priests ,
which I eject from my body--

My body that I don't like so much,
but I don't mock it as it should be mocked.
Or love it as it should be loved.

I never sip drowsiness all at once ,
didn't think of seeking it
from the shepherds' Sheikhs.
And I didn't learn the rules of love
before falling asleep.
I used to feel bored by Rumi's speeches,
and I like to think of death as a mistress.

A mistress won't repeat :
Must, must, must.
A mistress won't say :
Follow me ,
oh sheep of the Lord,
to the grassy hillock I'll show you .
A mistress doesn't love
inadvertently or negligently .

A mistress wont swing like a gallows
nor wrap around like a snake

when she pursues you
through punctuation marks ,

the mistress you chose to name
another name
like the detritus of a stray spider--
Do I say "the mistress" a lot?

My body is in pain ,
and I don't take care of myself.
My eyes can't adjust to the darkness.
I don't care about your answer .

You are suffocated like another beat
in a theatrical rhythm.
There is no genetic mutation rising
in the twilight of the trail.

Only the mistress
is spinning surreptitiously
the carpet for marching .
...

3-Lust

I keep lust in the flames of my heart,
but its fragrance strips the secrets
of the nebula's pulse .

The fragrance is the language
of the stolen senses in the cave .
It doesn't show its self-celebration
even to its owner - the host.
She tells him to cheer up
or be more humble or angry.
And anger,
it deludes him with his heroism
and superiority when he feels it.

The perfect wetness for a cat's nose
doesn't suit the repetition
of your dry cheeks.

The smell is its silent language
and our luminous lust,
and we are dependents,
nothing but dependents ,
on the ether .
...

4-A Hole of "NO"

In searching for freedom, seeps
in the inverted "NO"
as a mode of blending
for another rhythm .

Certainty is doubt, sung in a choir.
Doubt is the certainty
of the nihilism of assertion
and the imperative melody .

Your highest ideal grows up
--without your notice--
like a dry sapling,
mocking the obesity of the axe.
And I am trying to smash it
with your right hand
while your left hand is busy
kneading the last clay
as it falls like fresh, ripe dates
and seeds with discomforted vision
between your fingers.
...

5-Thirst

I have a permanent thirst
and craving for a river
that knows very well the braids
of its delta .
It has no knowledge of Adam
and understands nothing
from the Bible of wetness
but the verse of the seventh swan.

It found its lord in this
and realized that it, itself, was the lord's desired element .

The verse is a watery virtue.
Its sweetness means that
an elegant creature of salt
is dancing devoutly between the waves .

The Lord didn't tell me
to put my hand around her waist,
but he was peeping through
the moon holes .
I think he loved it like me
because it was haunted by
the Meningitis of kisses .

The kiss is a furrow in the lips--
the spring breath from it,
its casual Arabic existence ,

and bleeding is a young lady
who speaks French fluently,
better than any authentic Francophone
or any European, strangled
with the entrails of a priest
on a pure collar,
its Arabism not yet dried up.
...

6-The Peak

Why do you think of another peak
when you summit your own mountain,
and why do you become infected by vanity
and practice laughing
while there is no one to listen
to the flight of Ecstasy .

Lionizing is a naive social creature ;
in loneliness, laughing become nothing but a buzz.

Your foot is still touching the dirt ,

and the peak is not an ideal end
for a superior variety .

The peak is the starting line in the race--

You just need to smile and feel
the vitality .

You will leap and bet on flying
with all the weight of your letters .

And what if you fall? Your soul
won't touch the desert .

And your body will reach its highest condition while it is falling ,
crushed by the humility of your bones against nature .

The air feels you ;
drizzle wishes to write your blood's Iliad

and feels proud when it reads it
and asks itself: is it really me
who wrote the elegy of bleeding ?

Reading is rewriting after liberation
from the Obsession of membranes.

It is a pure framing for the last jump--
a frame, but a part of the intimacy of creation.
....

7-Beards

And I see
sometimes
henna beards and clothes, sticks
hunting a wolf that loses blood.
And when the wolf thinks,
he becomes human.
And when red beards think,
they become an expected error
in an ancient chemical law.

The wolf worships the howl.
He thinks what it has to say
and how he will get angry
and scream in the tongue of the master
between every verse of reverence
and the verses that retrace his way
back to the pack's behavior.

When henna thinks,
time says nothing
but chants of a weak stick.
 ....

8-Sons of Clay

When the sons of clay cheer:
You, you, you and you,
I didn't become prouder .
It is not my habit
to wear
a rosary for humility ,
made of gemstones .

And I don't lionize the body
or sing to it.

And I don't say "I" to feel the value
of difference
and its spiritual beauty .

Speaking is a vocal act.

And the Different is a necessary exciting of stillness

that doesn't need an indication
by a side effect ,
nor a side reaction
when the Vanity gets stained
by the details of the body .

The Vanity is not a sin
as much as a reaction .

I prefer to be the language of the spring,
rather than being the ratio of the aperture
in a remnant mobile's pupil .
...

9-Feminization

I don't need the feminine pronoun
to redefine Virility.

The sun is immanent and solid enough
to evade the temptation of shadow .

Needing to be defined
is like the act of mocking others.
It is the real parity.

Parity is a behavior, not a description --
a behavior that is not suitable
with knowledge, nor with the vanity
that wears certainty ,
which is above everything
because we cannot define it
as a peer of stupidity .
...

10-Tidings

I bring you glad tidings
of death's sweetness,
and bury my laughter as a soulful crow.

Death absorbs
the activated charge
for a wish's obstruction.

The dream's implications
are not effective without
fertility.

Death is an active fertility.
It is the temporary motivation ,
an opportunity that won't be repeated.
Only death
doesn't end with death
and begin with life.

I bring you tidings of a Praiseworthy death ,
and a Praiseworthy ambition ,

and a resignation that kills
the limited ambition
by the abiosis of the obsession of seeking,
a resignation that makes its glory
as slow as a sculptor
on the liquid scriptures of eternity.
...

11-The Shyness of Hatred

Why should I choose you as an enemy?
I didn't contemplate you;
why should I envy you
while my tongue doesn't remember your name?

I don't love you
because I didn't think of hating you.
I don't hate you
because I don't see you.

Hatred, like shyness, is a temporary reflex
for a scent of a fate.

Reflex is an instinct for a human being;
preventing it is a reflex, too,
that might be confused with a solid pulse --
a pulse shielded by flowing
like a river that does not contemplate the stable stones to ignore them.

It is the unconditional flow,

a flow inspired from within.
...

12-Supreme Authority

Why do you need a supreme authority
to monitor how many times you cleaned your urethra and anus with water,
and trying to rationalize the wetness in your lips,
it thinks about you as an individual element of a collective behavior
but it wastes grand springs from your eyes
and buries a sea of pulsing avicennias.

So Excess is what I bring you as a tiding.
Excess is similar to death.
Excess is the dream of not needing a dream jacket.

It is jumping a quarter tone on the melody while singing,
like spilling colors on a painting
in a smear of delight.

Workers compulsively cut
from the insurance of their sweats
letters for an unknown recipient.
So what if they donate half of a tear voluntarily?
The accumulation of half tears can repair tin houses,
spread out like a lazy banana leaf.

Excess is the only truth of our faith.

And let some of you call it the stolen revolution
of *Animal Farm* as a rhythmic narrative.

Let some of you call it a trace

of a nightly knapsack and the crumbs of dialog.
And all of you should call it a -----------
---------------------- ------------------------
-----* from what an accent of silence hides
in the lisp of knowledge,
which you cannot understand at its core,
except by creating a movement in the vacuum.

...
*Censored by the Supreme Authority

13-Forgetting

While you are in the cave,
won't you forget the weight of the mountain's breaths?
Won't you forget the tired steps
of the times when they trample the thorns of the grass?
While the stones of minuets fall from them
with the scream of conventions,

won't you forget the dung beetles
that breed in the stinking water,
wrapping gifts for their females
in their fertilizing balls?

The female you forgot
was not a woman,
but a pure waste of a delayed craving,
and a culture of a desire that could be matured.

When you remember,
write your anticipation
on the scraps of the wind.
From the scent of the dung, pick
musk pheromones; then tame them, and call them.
They will come to you as awareness.

There exists a sexual desire between musk and defecation,
similar to a craving for chocolate while reading.

Your desire is against impartiality.
When you remember,
say: Oh, good insect,

your nose is tall and wise.
And those sticky insects
which eat your grass after a busy day
have a snubbed nose
or one hooked like an internal agenda.

Say: Oh, good insect,
your millionth grandmother was hit
by the windshield of a car
owned by a bug who was addicted to Tango
and didn't pay attention to your eternal sadness.

When you remember,
don't fall downhill
on the lungs of chaos.

Rather, give the resonance
its freedom to be free
from the waste and the deep,
fatal wakefulness,

for this cave
doesn't care about the eternity of the mountain,
nor its skill in coexistence with
a pole fascinated by stripping.
...

14-Lionizing

I am thinking
about my pain --
no one shares it with me.

And about my joy --
I don't partake of it with passersby,
and it runs away from my fingers every time.

I lionize my pain
for no reason, but because
it belongs to me.

I cannot smile well,
and the wind encourages me to jump
to where I can't see.

The gnat
knows how to jump,
how to mock the wind
when it takes an aerial step back,
then smuggles a smile under its wings.
And like you, I prefer the refraction
instead of being like a gnat
or anything on its back.
...

15-The Secret Ejaculation of a Chestnut

What does it mean
if you prevent yourself from practicing the peeper habit
while you are sniffing the chestnut's sent
in the details of your body?

Your eyes will become sharper
when they weave the details of the argument,
hunted by avoidance as a daily behavior.
And the corpse of your object of virtue
as intellectual behavior
in all your body's tremors,
ejaculating your thoughts in its libidinous form,
deceives by pouring the inspiration
to be free from the complex
of the absolute power.

Be Al-HurrAr-Riyahi when you choose
carefully the size of your shackle,
exaggerating in the rituals of reverence
at the moment of liberation by it.
Only freedom deserves your servitude.
Your back hunches bashfully
while you are washing yourself with the marshes of tears
like the blade that lived in your heart,
beginning with new blood
or a blood recycled one second after
the moment of the vision.
...

16-A Universal Corridor

When I closed my eyes,
the universe passed through me completely
in a second -- or a little less.

All those invisible particles
chose me as a corridor to the side of theorization,
bragging by their differences,
its different formation, its impressive product,
its tyranny in making an embodiment of goodness
or the capability of inventing evil,

unaware that they tried to speak
with a different accent of a language migrated to the crushed past,
tried like virtual tribes lost their tent stakes,

unaware that they are a pure orphaned word
named Love --
or something similar to it:

Love as a thought of a concept and a seed of assent;

Love as a knife of peace and flowers of a torturing spring;

Love as a catalyst of smoke and an inhibitor of an odor;

Love as a color of a gesture and a shade of a sign.

When you realize that
you can't be devoted to love as a value

nor as an icon of a digital biography
for the potential of hydrogen in an individual behavior,

then Evil is not the soppiest of good;
it is the eternal integration
of the system and its clotted surrounding,
when a universe has been created
by fingertips of Love.
...

17-A Midwife's Mirror

Look beyond the mirror, and you will find pure love.
Look at the mirror's body, and you will find safe company.
Look at the mirror's silver,
and you will find the relatives,
hanging with the towel.

Glittering is self-made,
an unremunerated cleaning curator
when you deal with your language
as a professional football player
in a yard that has no grass with integrity,
keeping your balance in an emptied march
without any bundle of feelings,

smiling with the glittering.

And without any bundle of feelings,
you obey with amiably.

And without any bundle of feelings,
you love.

The mirror is smiling.
When you see your shadow smiles,
while it ignores
your craving in the time of smiling.

This mirror is to become a computer network for correlation

with feedback factors

without a headache
or reserving a storage for meditation,
for curiosity or reaction.

The mirror is a safe company.

Beyond the mirror is a phase of searching --

Searching is a passionate correlation with perspective.

The perspective is a friend, formed like a mirror
that doesn't care about the angle of your shadow reflection,
and your shadow - as you know - is your only legacy
to the inheritance of the crucifixion.
...

18-Standard Girl

The girl plays with dolls
and makes a romantic dialog
like a quilt from her grandmother's tales
that doesn't satisfy your taste.

You need a girl that takes a relish in plucking dolls' heads
and breaking toys' legs.
When you fight her for the flowing of her fabricated device,

this girl doesn't see you as a big child
deserving to be spoiled,
as someone lost sensing the simplicity of a color.

This girl sees you as
a challenging phase in this RPG game.

This girl can tame you when you think recklessly.

This girl doesn't carry a whip and sickle,
but can wear your skin violently
after she enjoys flaying it.

Yet she plays with you
the game of tea and dolls
to test your patience
and tells you about her need to go shopping
by mentioning all the details
and possible causes
in that certain time
and that certain day

to measure your endurance.

Be ready to indulge in your surrender
when she will have no mercy on you.
But --

When your girl forgets to taste your body,

leave... and think only about the viper.

Only the viper understands the essence of females.
The others are an escape that shuts the eyes of truth
with an eyelid's cacophony.

Escape the writing of an irreconcilable history.
...

19-Exaltation

While you are in your lonely exaltation,
like the last ascending exhalation of angels' smoke
looking for a partner,
extend your hand like a rod of light.
Then put your hand around the waist of
the first temptation of any fish
that can fly through your fingers.

Pull her to the chest of seduction.
Seduction is an anger pleasant in appearance.
Seduction is your gift to a concubine.
Perhaps her silver is her craft.

Don't think about fishing now,
not the glittering.
Think of your hand and the heavenly emptiness,
the winds fondling the dermis of the smile
and the wetness formed by a single drought
in a language turned into crumbs of clay --

A trembling clay,
like her waist
while it prepares itself
for a bustle banquet.
...

20-A Whip of Delight

And because you
cannot be exalted to become
indifferent or
to unite in oneness with annihilation,

tame yourself with the webs of joy.
Tame the one who hates you
by dinging his mocking wine with him.

Pour a whip of smile in your wine
and two whips of laughter.

Be aware of blessing that lowest of the mean
with the jewel of anger,

because anger is your precious treasure.

No one deserves it
but the one you love
when he does not rise with your breath
to the seduction of the mountain
while you are making love with the salt
in his body.

Anger is similar to love,
except it is more valuable.
It is an awareness of the details of the body
and its emotional loneliness --
And that is the first degree in the levels of ascension.
...

21-You Have No Limit

Think of death
as the curtain of a vintage theater.

Think of the dropping of the curtain
as the most important act of the dramatization of the text.

The limit of transcendence
is reaching the peak of an old mountain
and getting distracted by planting a flag
instead of flying.
So --
Don't die with transcendence
to be commemorated by others.

Die to be their autobiography.
Die in your last moment of life
because your presence, your absurdity and your smile
are parts of the transcendence system you're creating.
Transcendence is a pure degree of elevation associated with
towering.

Reaching is not your goal,
so create a path to pave
with the wrinkles of your soul.

That is a goal that couldn't be liquified
by aging.

Let the space open for vows of those committed to your
enlightenment.

Leave to your exaltation the sedition to provoke every potential highness

Oh, greatest Apathetic --
Don't turn back to death.
If you turn back,
you will see it,
exhausted but cheering you
because you are giving him an honorable life
and an ability to die quietly.
...

22-Not Defined

The definition is the deception of the behavior.
Behavior is the deception of the silent adjective.

The silent cannot exist by the language of the saying.
The saying doesn't need an identifier

Why are you practicing good behavior as a walking sport of Irfan
and sucking the sugar from the gum of time?
Sugar is like curious shells,
like the sea that doesn't stimulate the appetite of amygdalae in your brain,

addicted to the feeling of refreshment,
explaining to yourself that it is because of tiredness.

Read while moving your leg for another step.
What you see in the city
manifests itself in your body,

and what the others see
paints the lamppost in its dullness.
Dullness is its only virtue,

but the sophistication of color and stereotypical memory
is your purest virtue --
a virtue that you don't practice to redefine a yearly definition,
but to continue trying to eradicate it from the digital concept
of your potential being.
...

23-Wisdom is Foam

The foam
extends its middle finger
toward the stars.
The moon's snow is a melting mockery.

Whenever its quiet sign rises up,
it looks smaller.
The foam gets wiser when it wears the wind
and more modest
when she sheds her skin.
And you who are possessed by the lyricism of the scent
failed to notice the simplicity of the wisdom,
searching for the relationship
between time and color.

24-Texture of the Soul

My fingers are feeling
your achiness when you hallucinate,
feeling your breath's cheeks
when they turn their deaf ears
to the language of destruction
in the moan of annihilation
between your feet.

The weak obscures his sense of sight
and doesn't care about what his nose says to the lens of the shutter.

Only the exalted one
harkens -- as a shy student -- to the knife
and answers like an endless wound.
His truth contaminates the blade,
practicing the sport of terrorizing
the sparkling.

And the strong absorbs like an operatic boxer
every fist with his incisor,
staggering with a sly smile,
then rising before five in the morning.

He doesn't need to flow like a reaction;
he behaves naturally
as the last black piano key,
reciting the liturgy of the wind.

The strong is exalted,

but not solid
like the old Moustache thinks --
Not solid at all.

How many drops are enough to twist
a rock?!
....

25-Nothingness

You break free from the chords of time's joints,
and the goal evades the shackles of falling

to bring perfection to creation,
which means that you can perfectly create the nothingness

and realize the essence of the fallen marbles
from the fingers of the sculptor before his suicide,

resurrected as a baby in every clear labor,
and come to a settlement with his growth inside you
and the cry of his cells in every extension.

The state of attraction that narrows with memory
absorbs the light wrinkles from your skin.
Darkness has its ways
that pulsate on the hills of your hands,

dry up like a river of language
in the classical woods of words.

There is no shadow for the truth,
and the truth wafts as an energy of intimacy
from the stringed coincidence.
...

26-Scatter of Chanting

My blood is a chorus of priests
chanting the hymn of revival,
embodying the reality of living immersion in yearning.

And when the cells exercise reverence,
the boys of heaven leave you.

You might need a new contaminated blade
to be stabbed by surprise
when time coagulates
and you are leaking out of your holes.

Warmth
is not an evidence of a pulse,
and flowing is not a synonym
for life.

Rising above
means drawing your own red line in a different direction,
not violated by beings of space
nor by the warmth of the salt that desired its blood.
...

27-Elite Dance

They dance three meters away
from the meeting line between
the insight and the net of your iris,

wearing the clothes of the silence that went dry
when your body passed by them.

Perhaps it was their unbridled desire for serenity.

Perhaps it is an aversion to a fleeting turbidity of carbonation.

When you look,
the curtain of rhythm does not drop,
but the desire
may become paralyzed.

To be theorizing,
you must share with the waves their deserting longing.
Words suffocate the chirping;
their smell violates the prayers of the body,
and silence is a fleeting moment
that loses its ice with lowering
the rhythm of the departure's Dabke.

Think about the breadth of your eyes that provoke the ether,
and your bad time interfering with the pulse,
and your sharp smile as a letter in the end of the light pigment,
and how it makes you - somehow -
desirable.
....

28-The First Mud

Look for another silt stain
to wash off the questions,

a sin of a show
that does not absorb the scent of water from the breaths of people passing by
nor listens to the confusion of dust in their whispers.

Mud has its transcendent wisdom.
It penetrates you like an eternal fishing hook
and hardens like a labyrinth's wrinkles.

Mud has its style
in stimulating slipping behaviors
and accessing the spirituality of the truth
and its stony knowledge.

The mud has its climbing creatures.
They remind you of the mud.
They violate with a spray of language and return you to mud
when they hang like halogen grapes
and deprive you of it.

The mud has its little loaves, night lamps,
slippery clothes, wishes shaped like small balloons
and bags of dried roses,

a red signal that does not lose the cotton of its color,
a twilight without a body
or illumination.
...

29-The Woodenness of a Letter

When you become a branch,
you won't get caught up with the thought
of the woodenness of the bark.

You live in your soul and your heartbeat,
burying yourself with your self.

Greatness is when you do not acknowledge your
transcendence.
Transcendence is a state of swimming,
and pure stillness
is crystallizing the salt of knowledge.

Your shiver is your negation and your weakness.
Your shiver is an outpouring of beauty
from the sponge holes and water cells
like a dull epistaxis.
There are no fig leaves present in your scent,
nor enlightenment in a cluster of berries,

emptied of the desire for light and darkness
and the pleasure of growing shadows at the time of the escape,

emptied of your superiority.
And you like that.
...

30-Masks

Put on your mask.
This face that wears you
is worse than the disclosure.

You need to master the sport of lying
and train the calmness of the algae dye
in the cheeks of your lips to fabricate
the naivety of believing
and paste the weeds of manhood
over your objectionable smile.

The choicest wine of maturity
is absorbing the seeds from the intimacy of the grass,
condensing green jelly
in the leaves of dryness.

What if you selectively pick a natural pheromone
to mate with a plastic tree.
Maybe a song will blossom
after the nail polish has its vacation
from her last academic year.

Feminine maturity is another supremacy of the movement of time
and a noble wound to the flank of Arabized history.
...

31-Panting

I can't listen well to the opera of cawing,
but I can understand its music.
It has a classic ritual like a pre-Islamic poem
that did not dwell yet in Hell.
Hands took up her loaf
in an imported bamboo Sufi dance.

You don't need to stare at her.
Your ear does not widen as wide as your pupil,
and your heart will not be able to translate
the minutes of its oral scent.

There are no flames to kindle with it the desire of words,
nor does your imagination aid your stature when you imagine

only the effects of owls hissing.
Know how to erase your stutter
when you fall forward,
the dew of a young rose

flaunting the mastery of the paced quest.
And you know very well that innovation
may happen upon stumbling
before falling

and that is another degree of liberation
without rocking the whole-fat tails.
...

32-The Effects of Ravages

Waddling, overloaded with narration,
your right leg carries you on the sidewalk body
and your left takes the job of
scattering the traces of absurdity.

You are good at selecting
your own language
at every reflection of an eye
or refraction of scent by the synonyms of greetings
and what you wore of humpback rainy coats.

You fall down the side of the possible
as a spinal disc herniation in the rhythm
and huddle yourself with crutches of imagination.

Your lisps are purer than you,
and your impairments
-- those you choose to brag about every time -
are the gate of your ascension.

You pick a poison fit for life
and place the snake/ your female
in the fabric of the shirt of time.

Time is your only concern
and your only salvation.

Wound it by the silent will
before thrombosing.

The blue time
Al
ways
Eva-po-rates.

33-Reluctance

You endow the river with the reluctance of being warped by the glory of the flowing,
abstain from biting the corpse of the clay carcass inside of you.

You love more than accepting the grass hymn,
less confident from
the gasping of the salt beneath your feet.

You desire more than
~~taking care of dew-made breasts~~
~~You have more pride than~~
paying attention to downstream language or flowing revolution
~~of the trinity of life that steeps in language~~.

The revelation of the heart ~~feminized inside you~~
~~and reproduces around you~~ with young pulses,
~~with her new clothes~~ and ~~her~~ (his) just-washed hair,

writing about your satisfaction ~~on every sheet of eye~~,
about being humble with reckless people,
and about your humility with boys of fortune.

~~But contentment is not behavior.~~
~~Contentment is the absolute parallel;~~
it is the core of the horizon
and the earth's flat hands.

Don't sip ~~the shyness of the vines,~~
~~the shiver of the jugulars~~
~~nor the brown sugar in~~
the music of the language.
…..

34-Pleasure

I get pleasure from the fruits of narration I possess
with a thought of the vine's cluster,
scars of the gods' rain,
an old, curdled peel
or a fermentation of a new wish.

I get pleasure from what is coming
and from what I don't know about it,
that desired nonexistent thing
with all of its details.

My body is a Pandora's jar.
Blood is a gulf that bleeds its joy.
I preserve what remains of the tragedy
like bracelets of local identity and manufacture
sold at a foreign scrap market.
...

35-Single god

It is a habit:
roses wither;
writers stop walking at the paper platform.
And I don't care about the wind's games schedule
in the second division.

I might be practicing tap dance as a postmodern art
without anticipation of its inevitable manifestation
on a thin computer screen.

I have one god,
a lot of infidel thoughts,
followers who are not good at reciting anything
except the letters of Zār,
and disciples who are shackled by the longing and dreariness --

dreariness that is no longer alone,
nor has changed very much.

I don't pour myself into the heart of the lung.
I do not hide myself as a squirrel's treasure
or a guardian master's bone attentive to the clouds.

Precaution is another barrier to the loss of memory
Precaution is the lost, the impossible dream.

Spontaneous experimentation
is my only language for interrogating life.
...

36-New Wool

My skin,
averse from the coats of contentment,
will get red spots
in its spine
when the coat scratches him
with its gentle claws.

My lungs,
averse to the smell of lacking ambition,
have a desire that is freed from the wool of questions,
and I don't need the crutches of expectation nor sentinel
needles.

Walking and playing solo
is my secret weapon.
Probably
I need extreme selfishness again.
I am not thinking
of devising a modern physical definition
for my fingers ache ambitious
and tremble
with every drop of my heart

I might reap the dream
after another inflammation of the thumb.
...

37-Elevation

The way is lonely
if you look at the cloud stairs,

lonely and spacious for a traveler to get lost in
or to stand dancing like a flame between flying beings.

I need more lift
than a feather's ability to skate
in order to dispense with air oxidized by dry silicon
in water tattoos.

My ego has eight layers,
like a guest's modesty in hesitating to request a hot bath
bucket.

I need Tuaregs who are good at reading the caches of sand.
And perhaps they can transmit the prophecies
for narrators who are good at knocking on the sky with pegs of
light.

The elevation's trick
is to look up
when up is another down.

The center of light
is the only direction of prostration,
and prostration is my organic key
and displaced lock.

My heart is knotted

on life's riverbank.
It flows indifferent to your agglomeration
on a clean and classy orphan edge.
...

38-Whirlwind

You write superscript prose.
It stirs up a whirlwind of flying question marks and amazement.
Erase a point from contentment's commas
while you are searching for the essence of the search.

Your journey is a permanent goal,
your peregrinations a life.

As for your existence, it is an eternal toss.
Saving others
is not the beat of your soul
because peace is not your language
in speech.

You knot your symbol, not to be deciphered
but for the other to realize
his ability to expose the transparency of the knot
and untying the sequence bond of recitation.

The sun - the moon's only trick -
is good at manipulating the emotions of the sunset.
And when it makes a tablet,
it breaks a fresh one.

Salt is still your body,
and your ribs could be replaced with a new prism
or a vintage bottle of narration.
...

39-Sandy

Your time flows with the sand
in the moment of flipping the hourglass
with your dissolved feathers and dry cells.
It's your omission to count the manufactured standard kisses
before plunging into the flow.

How did you omit the inkwell?
And did you not indulge yourself in the feather of revelation?

How did you smuggle some of your immigrants with the shiver
of the morning
and the yawns of the waves' hands?

Your revelation is breakable.

This is how you must trust
the ability of your breath to resurrect
and format dances of sludge
in the boxes of old, stagnant water.
...

40-A Sense of Place

She passes by you,
sits on the opposite chair,
chooses another seated stranger,
and doesn't notice the loaf of your eyes.

Your pupils are fresh and hot
and ample for having breakfast with a family
that does not carry a cup of a lover
nor the warmth of a ginger tale.

You are preoccupied with a scent similar to her mate's coffee.
You evoke a place where you lived its memory
and a dance to whose rhythm you did not listen.

Your charm is a Mandaeism's baptism
smoking the jeremiad of jazz in a rolled joint of water

Thinking of a cigarette's lipstick
and the sewing of the tobacco, which you only occasionally
injected with marijuana,
in the reading clubs that celebrate balls of wool and meow

forgetting which lip's angle
can enhance hugging the roll with a lover's precision
and which tobacco did you store for bold political delirium?

Her hair is gypsy poetry.
So why don't you consider the temptation of your revelation
as any young girl would!
...

41-Leadership

March to the sea
with the conscious intent of a gull
that willfully neglected to join the flock.

The waves are trotting like your words with the wind,
and patience gets bored with your lack of interest.

Its cravings don't tempt you to hunt a hypothetical butterfly,
nor does its arrogance satisfy
when your pulse is released as a ray,
proved by the void.

You look like a mass death.
You don't repeat worn out questions.
You do not say: *Am I the one now sailing in the sea
or is the sea sailing me?* thinking you are practicing smart action,

and you don't completely underestimate the notion of the violated suffix in the poem,

reconciling with yourself, uniting with it
as an instinct formed before birth,
trying to preserve itself
in all this nonsense spanning the vastness of the universe
in a cup of water.
Its empty half is your
homeland.
...

42-Theft

You steal honey from a bear's mouth that has been crushed with hazelnuts
in the moment of hibernation

and suck the sweat of the middle classes' stomachs
from the bee camps.

Your mouth is full of shattered wax.
Your language is the mowing of the grass,
scattered from your lips.

You are neither completely yellow nor a clever triangle creature,
and you're not a dull square.

You never disgust anyone,
but your stick
recoils disgusted at the monotonous mooing,

and your heart does not care about an oozing flower
or the buzz of an old lumberjack

violating every shadow of a seedling.
And your transgression curses the sun.

You have a belt of neutrality.
What is Neutrality?!

Is it not a search in the cold
for a vegetarian coat

never thinking of the heat of the morning breeze?

Is there an odor that is not stolen when an example's stick is burned?
Would it exist if it had not been raped
by a stray nose?!

Your being is similar,
and your stick doesn't care about sand supplications,
nor do the vanities of the skin beings that look like you.

When the left hand denies the right-hand's ability
to sing solo with a sixth chord
and excel in jumping the possible rope in the throat

Fire snitches on you,
and Hell can only be attained by transcendence,
honorable, and mighty
like you.
...

43-Absorption

You don't need to absorb grammar
in the conversation of organic corn
or look at the rewritten genetic code
to know the genealogy of the soul and the race of the pulse
and its first tribes at the beginning of the writing and
classification of reproduction,
nor to measure how well the back can hold a shoe size
when you tried to slide to a branch on another page.

There is a genetic leap of faith in the prose
that makes a difference to your poetry growth
and an annoying disorder in the stomach of the poem.

Damn both of us.

Your seeds are not valid
for the upcoming generation
nor for the elders
because the voices of the multiple gods
in your brain's temple
are struggling with my survival.

What if the elderly voice crushed
the young testicles?

What if your virgin feminine hesitation committed suicide
before the final Friday night dialogue?

What if your childish voice gets bored
of the crying doll?
...

Made in United States
Orlando, FL
11 June 2024